Brain Power

Brain Power

Unlocking the Secrets of Learning and Memory

B. Vincent

QuantumQuill Press

CONTENTS

Introduction   1

1 | Chapter 1: Brain Anatomy and Function   4

2 | Chapter 2: Neuroplasticity   7

3 | Chapter 3: Memory Systems   10

4 | Chapter 4: Cognitive Neuroscience of Learning   13

5 | Chapter 5: Effective Learning Techniques   17

6 | Chapter 6: Lifestyle Factors That Affect Brain Health   20

7 | Chapter 7: The Role of Emotion and Motivation in Learning   24

8 | Chapter 8: Learning in the Digital Age   27

9 | Chapter 9: Lifelong Learning and
Brain Aging   30

10 | Chapter 10: Practical Applications
and Case Studies   33

Reflecting on the Journey   36

Appendix A: Glossary of Terms   39

Introduction

Embracing the Power Inside

Envision having a device so strong that it could change your fantasies into the real world, your inquiries into responds to, and your considerations into manifestations. This device doesn't lie in the outer world however inside your own brain. It is your cerebrum - the most mind boggling and glorious organ in the human body. At the core of each and every choice, memory, learning, and inventive undertaking, the mind organizes a multifaceted expressive dance of neurons and neurotransmitters, empowering us to explore the intricacies of the world.

However, in general, this amazing potential remaining parts to a great extent undiscovered. The mysteries of expanding learning and bridling the full limit of memory are frequently darkened by legends and deception. During a time where data is bountiful however insight is scant, understanding the genuine capacities of your intellectual prowess is the way to opening an existence of upgraded learning, further developed memory, and higher mental working.

This book, "Intellectual prowess: Opening the Mysteries of Learning and Memory," is your manual for demystifying the intricacies of the mind and uncovering the methodologies that can prompt upgraded mental capacities. Through the investigation of weighty logical exploration and the utilization of demonstrated learning strategies, you will find how to hone your brain, work on your memory, and change the manner in which you make the most of every situation.

The Excursion Ahead

The excursion through the pages of this book is one of revelation and strengthening. By understanding how your mind functions, you open the possibility to further develop your learning proficiency, hold data longer, and apply information all the more really. Whether you are an understudy taking a stab at scholastic greatness, an expert trying to remain ahead in a serious climate, or basically somebody with a hunger for deep rooted learning, the bits of knowledge gave here will be significant.

Our investigation will take us through the central standards of mind life systems and the neuroplastic idea of learning and memory. We will dig into the mental neuroscience behind how we learn, disentangle the memory frameworks that oversee how we hold data, and analyze the effect of way of life decisions on our mental well-being. Besides, we will examine the profound and inspirational parts of getting the hang of, understanding what they mean for our capacity to process and recall data.

Furnished with this information, we will present a progression of successful learning procedures and techniques intended to upgrade your review propensities, upgrade memory maintenance, and work on mental execution. From proof based rehearses like divided redundancy and elaborative cross examination to the job of nourishment, exercise, and snooze cerebrum wellbeing, you will figure out how to saddle the full force of your mind.

As we move past hypothesis into viable application, you will find how to adjust these procedures to the difficulties and chances of the computerized age. We will investigate the idea of deep rooted learning and the significance of keeping up with mental essential-ness as we age. Genuine contextual analyses will show how people and networks have effectively applied these standards to accomplish amazing enhancements in learning and memory.

Enabling Your Mental Excursion

This book is in excess of an assortment of realities and techniques; it is a source of inspiration. In understanding the mysteries of learning and memory, you are outfitted with the apparatuses to roll out significant improvements in your day to day existence. The way to improved intellectual prowess isn't without its difficulties, requiring commitment, steadiness, and an eagerness to try. However, the prizes are unlimited, prompting a really satisfying, useful, and mentally lively life.

As you leave on this excursion, recollect that the mission for information is a deep rooted experience. The techniques and experiences introduced here are not the last word but rather venturing stones toward a more profound comprehension of your mental capacities. The genuine capability of your mind is restricted simply by your obligation to development and learning.

With each page, you will draw nearer to opening the mysteries of your cerebrum, growing the limits of your learning, and accomplishing a degree of memory and mental capability you might have thought inconceivable. Welcome to the excursion that could only be described as epic, an excursion into the core of intellectual prowess.

The Way ahead

As we adventure forward, let every part act as a guidepost, enlightening the way to improved mental capacities. Keep a receptive outlook, be prepared to challenge your biases, and plan to embrace the procedures that will change your way to deal with learning and memory. The insider facts of your mind anticipate, and with them, the ability to transform you.

1

Chapter 1: Brain Anatomy and Function

Understanding the frontal cortex's life designs and capacity is essential to opening the secrets of learning and memory. The human frontal cortex, a confounding and muddled organ, is the control focal point of the tangible framework and directs everything from fundamental life capacities to complex mental cycles. Here, we'll research the crucial plans of the frontal cortex and their positions in learning and memory.

The Development of the Frontal cortex

The psyche can be completely divided into three essential parts: the cerebrum, the cerebellum, and the brainstem.

The Cerebrum: The greatest piece of the frontal cortex, at risk for mental abilities like thinking, learning, memory, and bearing. It is isolated into different sides of the equator (left and right) and is also parceled into bends: forward looking, parietal, transient, and occipital, each with specific abilities.

The Cerebellum: Arranged under the cerebrum, its fundamental ability is to orchestrate obstinate turns of events, harmony, and position anyway it also expects parts in motor learning and mental capacities.

The Brainstem: Goes probably as an exchange local area communicating the cerebrum and cerebellum to the spinal string. It controls various irreplaceable abilities, including heartbeat, breathing, and rest cycles.

Key Locales Related with Learning and Memory

Hippocampus: Arranged in the transient bend, the hippocampus expects a crucial part in the improvement of new memories and is locked in with learning.

Amygdala: Moreover in the transient bend, it processes sentiments and is associated with both up close and personal learning and memory.

Prefrontal Cortex: A piece of the frontal cortex, it's locked in with bearing, decisive reasoning, and organizing, and expects a section in working memory.

Neocortex: This outer layer of the cerebrum is locked in with higher-demand frontal cortex works like material acumen, time of motor requests, spatial reasoning, and language.

How the Frontal cortex Cycles Information

The most widely recognized approach to learning and memory incorporates various advances: encoding, association, storing, and recuperation. These methods attract different bits of the brain:

Encoding: The hippocampus and enveloping normal common bend structures are fundamental for encoding new information.

Association: The communication by which brief, as of late academic information turns out to be consistent and long stretch. This incorporates both the hippocampus for unequivocal memories and the basal ganglia for procedural memories.

Limit: Information is taken care of across different, interconnected districts of the brain. The cortex expects a gigantic part in the really long storing of data.

Recuperation: Moving to information set aside in the psyche, which relies upon the hippocampus for applicable memories and the prefrontal cortex for working memory.

Neurons and Neurotransmitters

At the little level, the brain's capacities are finished by neurons, or nerve cells, which talk with each other through electrical and compound signs. This correspondence is worked with by neural connections, substance messengers that impart signals across synapses (the openings between neurons) to pass on information.

Synaptic Malleability: The limit of brain associations with sustain or weaken over an extended time, considering additions or lessens in their activity. This flexibility is the preparation of learning and memory.

The brain's life frameworks and ability are complicatedly associated with how we learn and recall. From the colossal degree structures like the cerebrum and cerebellum to the moment coordinated efforts among neurons and neurotransmitters, each part expects a crucial part in our intellectual abilities. Understanding these basics clears a path for examining how we can work on these cycles, a subject we'll dive into in the going with segments.

Chapter 2: Neuroplasticity

Cerebrum versatility

Cerebrum flexibility, generally called mind malleability or mind flexibility, implies the frontal cortex's ability to change and change all through a solitary's life. This adaptability is showed up in additional ways than one, including the advancement of new cerebrum affiliations, the period of new neurons, and the patching up of mind networks considering learning, experience, and injury. Cerebrum flexibility is the basis of our capacity to dominate new capacities, recover from mind wounds, and conform to new conditions or conditions.

Kinds of Cerebrum flexibility

•Fundamental Malleability: Essential adaptability suggests the frontal cortex's ability to really change its development in light of learning or experience. This recalls changes for the relationship between neurons, known as synapses, and changes in the dendritic branches and axons of neurons.

•Pragmatic Flexibility: Utilitarian flexibility is the frontal cortex's ability to move capacities from a hurt locale of the brain to unblemished districts. This kind of flexibility allows the brain to compensate for injury and adapt to new learning or environmental changes.

Instruments Behind Cerebrum versatility

•Synaptic Malleability: At the center of mind flexibility is synaptic adaptability, the limit of synapses (the signs of correspondence between neurons) to sustain or cripple after some time. Synaptic flexibility is crucial for learning and memory, as it impacts how actually neurons can talk with each other.

•Neurogenesis: Once acknowledged to be unimaginable in adults, neurogenesis, the most well-known approach to making new neurons, occurs in unambiguous locale of the psyche, similar to the hippocampus. This cycle is major for molding new memories and learning.

Factors Influencing Cerebrum flexibility

•Age: While cerebrum flexibility happens all through the future, it is more expressed in young people. Regardless, adults can moreover overhaul their frontal cortex's flexibility through various activities and experiences.

•Learning and Experience: Partaking in new learning works out, getting new capacities, and being introduced to various experiences advance mind versatility by vitalizing the course of action of new cerebrum affiliations.

•Work out: Real work deals with by and large as well as earnestly influences the frontal cortex. Practice propels neurogenesis and the appearance of neurotrophic factors, which support neuron improvement and synaptic flexibility.

•Diet and Food: An eating routine affluent in cell fortifications, omega-3 unsaturated fats, and various enhancements maintains mind prosperity and updates cerebrum flexibility.

•Rest: Agreeable rest is fundamental for cerebrum flexibility. During rest, the frontal cortex adjusts and consolidates memories, supporting learning and memory improvement.

Redesigning Cerebrum versatility

Understanding mind flexibility empowers us to embrace lifestyles and participate in practices that advance frontal cortex prosperity and mental ability. Coming up next are several methods to further develop mind flexibility:

•Relentless Getting: Testing the psyche with new information and capacities invigorates the plan of new mind processes.

•Genuine Action: Standard dynamic work helps mind ability and redesigns neurogenesis.

•Care and Reflection: Practices like consideration and thought can additionally foster focus, lessen pressure, and enliven mind flexibility.

•Brilliant consuming less calories: A sensible eating routine maintains mind prosperity and can deal with mental capacity.

•Social Association: Partaking in critical social collaborations quickens the psyche and supports mental prosperity.

Cerebrum flexibility offers a certain perspective on the psyche's capacity for change and improvement. By getting it and using the principles of cerebrum versatility, we can update our learning, memory, and for the most part intellectual abilities. This part features the meaning of taking on a lifestyle that upholds frontal cortex prosperity, enabling perusers to partake in practices that quicken mind versatility and advance durable learning and mental adaptability.

3 ▌

Chapter 3: Memory Systems

Grasping Memory Frameworks

The human mind houses complex frameworks to process, store, and recover data, making learning and review conceivable. Memory is certainly not a solitary element yet a star grouping of frameworks, each with interesting jobs and systems. These frameworks empower us to recollect previous encounters, learn new data, explore our current circumstance, and plan for what's in store.

Kinds of Memory Frameworks

•Tangible Memory: Tactile memory is the earliest phase of memory. It permits people to hold impressions of tangible data after the first upgrade has stopped. This super momentary memory endures from a negligible part of one moment to a few seconds and is fundamental for seeing a persistent and stable world.

•Momentary Memory (STM) and Working Memory: Transient memory goes about as an impermanent stockpiling framework for data we are as of now contemplating or handling. Working memory, a connected idea, includes the control of data held in transient memory, like taking care of a numerical statement in your mind.

STM normally holds data for around 20 to 30 seconds, while working memory limit is restricted to around 7 +/ - 2 things of data.

•Long haul Memory (LTM): Long haul memory is the mind's framework for putting away, making due, and recovering data for expanded periods. LTM can endure from minutes to a lifetime and has an apparently limitless limit. It is partitioned into unequivocal (revelatory) memory and verifiable (non-definitive) memory.

oExplicit Memory: This type includes cognizant review of data, realities, and encounters and is additionally partitioned into rambling memory (individual encounters and occasions) and semantic memory (realities and general information).

oImplicit Memory: Verifiable memory incorporates recollections of which we are not intentionally mindful, like procedural memory (abilities and assignments), profound affiliations, and molded reactions.

The Job of the Mind in Memory

Various pieces of the cerebrum assume critical parts in different memory frameworks:

•Hippocampus: Basic for the development of new express recollections and spatial memory.

•Amygdala: Associated with profound memory, improving the review of genuinely charged occasions.

•Cerebral Cortex: Stores complex semantic and wordy recollections, appropriating components across various cerebrum districts.

•Cerebellum and Basal Ganglia: Assume parts in procedural memory, adding to ability acquiring and propensity arrangement.

Memory Development and Review Interaction

Memory development includes three key cycles: encoding, stockpiling, and recovery.

•Encoding: The method involved with changing over insights into recollections. This can be impacted by consideration, redundancy, profound state, and associations with existing information.

•Capacity: The union and joining of encoded data into present moment or long haul stockpiling.

•Recovery: Getting to and bringing into cognizance the data put away in long haul memory.

Upgrading Memory Frameworks

Understanding the different memory frameworks takes into consideration designated systems to upgrade memory capability:

•Further developing Encoding: Strategies like elaborative practice, memory aides, and creating significant associations can upgrade the encoding of data.

•Reinforcing Capacity: Rehashed survey, divided reiteration, and guaranteeing satisfactory rest can assist with uniting recollections for long haul stockpiling.

•Working with Recovery: Work on reviewing data, showing others, and utilizing signs or settings related with the memory can further develop recovery proficiency.

The perplexing memory frameworks of the human cerebrum support our learning, personality, and communications with the world. By utilizing experiences into how these frameworks work, people can take on procedures to further develop their memory abilities, upgrading both individual and expert parts of their lives. Understanding memory entrances according to a logical point of view as well as offers reasonable applications for day to day existence, empowering us to carry on with additional educated and successful lives.

4 |

Chapter 4: Cognitive Neuroscience of Learning

Figuring out Mental Neuroscience

Mental neuroscience is a part of neuroscience that concentrates on the brain systems basic mental capabilities like learning, memory, consideration, and critical thinking. It overcomes any issues between the actual design of the cerebrum and the perplexing cycles of the psyche, utilizing different techniques and advances to investigate how mind movement associates with mental encounters.

The Brain Premise of Learning

Learning includes changes inside the cerebrum that take into consideration the obtaining, handling, and capacity of new data. This interaction is worked with by a few key regions:

•The Prefrontal Cortex: Engaged with chief capabilities, independent direction, and applying figuring out how to tackle issues.

•The Hippocampus: Assumes a vital part in the development of new recollections and the reconciliation of new and existing information.

•The Amygdala: Related with profound learning and connecting close to home importance to recollections.

•The Cerebellum and Basal Ganglia: Engaged with the mastering of coordinated abilities and propensities, individually.

Synapses and Learning

Synapses are substance couriers that communicate signals across neurotransmitters starting with one neuron then onto the next, impacting and directing growing experiences. Key synapses include:

•Dopamine: Related with remuneration and inspiration, dopamine's delivery during growing experiences builds up ways of behaving and makes them bound to be rehashed.

•Acetylcholine: Assumes a part in consideration and excitement, working with the encoding of new data.

•Glutamate: Engaged with synaptic versatility, glutamate is fundamental for long haul potentiation, an instrument for reinforcing synaptic associations and a principal cycle for learning and memory.

Advancements in Mental Neuroscience

Progressions in innovation have significantly improved how we might interpret the mind's job in learning:

•Practical Attractive Reverberation Imaging (fMRI): Permits scientists to envision dynamic cerebrum regions during mental assignments, showing where growing experiences happen.

•Electroencephalography (EEG): Measures electrical movement in the cerebrum, giving bits of knowledge into the planning of mental cycles connected with learning.

•Transcranial Attractive Excitement (TMS): Can upgrade or disturb cerebrum capability in designated regions, assisting with grasping the job of explicit mind locales in learning.

Speculations of Learning in Mental Neuroscience

A few speculations inside mental neuroscience make sense of how learning happens, including:

•Hebbian Hypothesis: Frequently summed up as "cells that fire together, wire together," this hypothesis suggests that synaptic associations between neurons fortify as they are enacted all the while.

•Prescient Coding: Recommends that the mind continually makes and updates expectations about the world, learning through the rectification of blunders among anticipated and genuine encounters.

•Connectionism: Underlines the job of brain networks in getting the hang of, recommending that complicated mental cycles emerge from the communications of basic units (neurons) inside the organization.

Upgrading Learning through Neuroscience

Grasping the mental neuroscience of learning offers reasonable applications:

•Customized Instruction: Bits of knowledge into mind capability can prompt customized learning systems that take special care of individual qualities and shortcomings.

•Neurofeedback: By giving constant criticism on mind movement, people can figure out how to control their mental cycles, upgrading concentration and learning productivity.

•Mental Enhancers: Examination into synapses and brain components might prompt the advancement of medications or mediations that upgrade learning and memory.

The mental neuroscience of learning gives a window into the perplexing cycles that empower us to learn and adjust. By unwinding the intricacies of how learning happens at the brain level, we can foster designated procedures to improve instructive strategies, upgrade mental capacities, and figure out the maximum capacity of the human cerebrum. This section has featured the significance of coordinating neuroscience experiences into commonsense applications, promising a future where learning is more proficient, customized, and open to all.

Chapter 5: Effective Learning Techniques

In the excursion to bridle the maximum capacity of our mental ability, it is critical to figure out successful learning procedures. These systems are not just about packing data into transient memory however about really upgrading our capacity to learn, comprehend, and hold information in the long haul. This section investigates proof based procedures that have been displayed to further develop learning results essentially.

Separated Redundancy

Separated redundancy use the mental dividing impact, where learning is separated into various short meetings over a more drawn out timeframe. This procedure is diverged from massed reiteration, where learning happens in a solitary, long meeting. Divided reiteration works by deliberately expanding the spans between survey meetings of a similar material, really building up memory maintenance and review.

•Execution: Use cheat sheets for new jargon or ideas, and survey them at expanding spans. Applications that utilization divided redundancy calculations can assist with computerizing this interaction.

Dynamic Review

Dynamic review includes effectively animating memory during the educational experience. Rather than latently perusing or inspecting material, students test themselves by reviewing the data without checking the text out. This method fortifies memory and improves the growing experience.

•Execution: In the wake of perusing a part of text, close the book or cover the notes and attempt to review the central matters or subtleties. Practice this by utilizing tests or cheat sheets without checking out at the responses first.

Elaborative Cross examination

Elaborative cross examination is a scrutinizing procedure used to develop understanding. It includes inquiring "how" and "why" inquiries regarding the material being mastered, empowering students to make associations between new data and existing information.

•Execution: For each new idea or reality, wonder why it is valid or the way that it interfaces with what you definitely know. This cycle supports incorporating new information with existing mental constructions.

Interleaved Practice

Interleaved practice includes blending various themes or subjects to further develop learning. This differentiations with impeded practice, where one subject or sort of issue is concentrated broadly prior to continuing on to another. Interleaving reinforces advancing by empowering the cerebrum to continually acclimate to new sorts of issues, upgrading critical thinking abilities.

•Execution: If concentrating on math, rather than rehearsing just a single kind of issue at a time, mix different sorts of issues in a solitary report meeting.

Double Coding

Double coding joins verbal and visual data to upgrade learning. By partner text-based data with visual guides, like outlines, graphs, or recordings, students can further develop review and understanding.

•Execution: While examining, go with your notes with applicable visuals. In the event that you're learning an idea, attempt to find or make a chart that delineates it. Whenever the situation allows, utilize both verbal and visual instructing materials.

The Testing Impact

The testing impact, otherwise called recovery practice, proposes that the demonstration of recovering data from memory improves and helps learning. Standard testing surveys information as well as builds up learning.

•Execution: Use practice tests routinely, not only for test arrangement. Self-testing or gathering tests can be powerful methods for building up learning.

These successful learning methods, upheld by mental science, offer amazing assets for upgrading learning and memory. By integrating these systems into your review schedules, you can essentially work on your capacity to learn, comprehend, and hold data. This part accentuates the significance of dynamic commitment with material, normal audit and testing, and the essential utilization of visual guides in learning. Taking on these procedures can prompt more productive and compelling getting the hang of, engaging you to accomplish your full mental potential.

Chapter 6: Lifestyle Factors That Affect Brain Health

The mission for improving learning and memory rises above past simple review methods and dives into the more extensive range of way of life decisions. The mind, an organ of dazzling intricacy, flourishes with specific circumstances to ideally work. This section investigates key way of life factors that assume a urgent part in keeping up with and improving cerebrum wellbeing, consequently in a roundabout way impacting our learning capacities and memory maintenance.

Sustenance

Sustenance holds a focal job in cerebrum wellbeing. The maxim "For getting healthy, the kind of food you eat is everything" reaches out to your cerebrum, influencing mental capability, memory, and by and large mind wellbeing. An eating regimen plentiful in cell re-inforcements, solid fats, nutrients, and minerals upholds cerebrum capability and safeguards against mental deterioration.

•Omega-3 Unsaturated fats: Tracked down in fish, flaxseeds, and pecans, omega-3s are fundamental for cerebrum wellbeing, helping with building mind and nerve cells critical for learning and memory.

•Cell reinforcements: Berries, nuts, and green verdant vegetables are high in cell reinforcements, which assist with combatting oxidative pressure and irritation, conditions that can add to mind maturing and neurodegenerative illnesses.

•Entire Grains: Food sources high in fiber, similar to entire grains, can further develop heart wellbeing, along these lines by implication supporting cerebrum wellbeing through superior blood stream.

Actual Activity

Practice isn't only advantageous for your body; it's likewise significant for your cerebrum. Standard active work builds the pulse, which siphons more oxygen to the mind. It likewise helps the arrival of chemicals, which give a climate helpful for the development of synapses.

•Neurogenesis: Exercise advances the development of new neurons in the hippocampus, a locale of the mind related with memory and learning.

•Stress Decrease: Normal actual work diminishes pressure and tension, conditions that can influence mental capability and memory.

Rest

Rest is a basic yet frequently disregarded part of cerebrum wellbeing. Sufficient tranquilizers in learning and memory in two vital ways: first and foremost, by assisting with combining recollections, consequently making them more grounded; and besides, by getting out poisons in the cerebrum that can influence mental capability.

•Memory Union: During rest, significant brain associations that structure our recollections are reinforced, and insignificant ones are pruned away.

•Cerebrum Detoxification: Rest initiates the glymphatic framework, which eliminates byproducts from the mind that collect during waking hours.

Mental Feeling

Participating in intellectually animating exercises keeps the mind dynamic and advances brain adaptability, the cerebrum's capacity to shape new brain associations over the course of life. This can be accomplished through mastering new abilities, leisure activities, or dialects, and by settling puzzles or participating in testing mental assignments.

•Mental Save: Exercises that challenge the mind fabricate a "mental hold" to assist the cerebrum with turning out to be stronger to harm that might happen with maturing.

Social Collaboration

People are intrinsically friendly animals, and ordinary social co-operation can significantly affect cerebrum wellbeing. Participating in significant discussions, taking part in friendly exercises, and keeping up with cozy connections can diminish pressure, avoid melancholy, and keep the brain sharp.

•Consistent encouragement: Solid social associations offer close to home help, which can lessen pressure and its destructive consequences for the cerebrum.

•Mental Commitment: Social collaborations frequently include complex mental cycles, like tuning in, thinking, and answering, which can animate mental capability.

Stress The board

Constant pressure can unleash ruin on the mind, influencing regions associated with memory and learning. Overseeing pressure through care, reflection, yoga, or other unwinding procedures can safeguard the cerebrum and upgrade mental capabilities.

•Decreasing Cortisol Levels: Elevated degrees of the pressure chemical cortisol can hinder mind capability, including memory and learning. Stress the board strategies can assist with bringing down cortisol levels and safeguard the cerebrum.

All in all, upgrading mind wellbeing through a comprehensive methodology enveloping sustenance, work out, rest, mental excitement, social collaboration, and stress the executives can fundamentally improve learning and memory. By embracing sound way of life decisions, people can uphold their mental capabilities, guaranteeing that their mind stays hearty and strong notwithstanding challenges, subsequently opening the maximum capacity of their intellectual ability.

Chapter 7: The Role of Emotion and Motivation in Learning

Feeling and inspiration assume basic parts in picking up, molding the manner in which we draw in with data and affecting our ability to hold and review information. This section dives into the many-sided connection between close to home states, persuasive drives, and the growing experience, offering bits of knowledge into how students can use these perspectives to improve their instructive results.

The Effect of Feeling on Learning

Close to home states significantly affect the educational experience. Positive feelings like interest, fervor, and interest can improve mental cycles, including consideration, memory, and critical thinking abilities. Alternately, gloomy feelings like nervousness, dread, and weariness can thwart these equivalent cycles, making learning seriously testing.

•Improving Positive Feelings: Techniques to cultivate good feelings in learning conditions incorporate making a steady and comprehensive air, consolidating components of gamification, and associating learning material to individual interests or true applications.

•Overseeing Gloomy Feelings: Methods to moderate pessimistic feelings incorporate care and stress-decrease works on, defining reasonable objectives, and looking for strong input.

Inspiration: The Main impetus Behind Learning

Inspiration is the main impetus that invigorates, coordinates, and supports conduct. With regards to learning, inspiration can be characteristic (driven by an interior craving to learn for individual fulfillment) or outward (determined by outside remunerations or tensions).

•Characteristic Inspiration: Cultivated via independence, authority, and reason, natural inspiration prompts further commitment and more relentless exertion in learning exercises.

•Extraneous Inspiration: While outward inspirations, for example, grades and rewards can be powerful temporarily, overreliance on them can sabotage characteristic inspiration. It is vital to Adjust these inspirations.

Methodologies to Upgrade Feeling and Inspiration in Learning

•Associate Figuring out how to Individual Interests: Making learning applicable to students' lives and interests can ignite interest and improve inspiration.

•Put forth Feasible Objectives: Setting clear, reachable objectives gives guidance and keeps up with inspiration through a feeling of progress and achievement.

•Develop a Development Mentality: Empowering a development outlook — the conviction that capacities can be created through commitment and difficult work — can support flexibility, inspiration, and accomplishment.

•Give Independence and Decision: Permitting students some level of decision in their way of learning can improve natural inspiration and commitment.

•Use Criticism Successfully: Valuable input assists students with figuring out their advancement and regions for development, filling in as a persuasive instrument for kept learning and improvement.

Profound and Persuasive Emotionally supportive networks

•Social Help: Advancing inside a strong local area can give close to home support and spur people through coordinated effort and shared objectives.

•Self-Guideline: Showing students self-guideline procedures, for example, objective setting, checking progress, and changing systems, engages them to assume command over their way of learning.

Understanding and utilizing the jobs of feeling and inspiration in learning can fundamentally upgrade instructive results. By encouraging positive close to home states, adjusting inherent and outward inspirations, and executing techniques that help profound prosperity and inspiration, teachers and students the same can make more viable and satisfying opportunities for growth. This part underlines the significance of tending to the profound and persuasive parts of getting the hang of, offering pragmatic guidance for developing a climate that sustains both the brain and the soul chasing after information.

8 |

Chapter 8: Learning in the Digital Age

The approach of advanced innovation has significantly changed the scene of instruction, offering new open doors for learning while additionally introducing extraordinary difficulties. This section investigates how advanced devices and stages are reshaping the manners by which we learn, the ramifications of these changes, and procedures to explore learning in the computerized age really.

The Development of Advanced Learning

Computerized learning incorporates a great many innovations and strategies, from online courses and virtual homerooms to instructive applications and advanced assets. The development of computerized learning has been portrayed by more prominent availability to data, adaptability in learning conditions, and customized opportunities for growth. Nonetheless, this development additionally requires decisive contemplating data sources and independent acquiring abilities.

•Openness: Computerized stages have made learning materials more available to a worldwide crowd, separating geological and financial hindrances to instruction.

•Personalization: Innovation empowers customized learning ways that adjust to individual students' assets, shortcomings, and speed, offering a more custom-made instructive experience.

•Intuitiveness: Computerized apparatuses work with intelligent growth opportunities, drawing in students through sight and sound substance, recreations, and gamification.

Open doors Introduced by Advanced Learning

•Deep rooted Learning: Advanced stages support long lasting getting the hang of, permitting people to secure new abilities and information all through their lives, paying little mind to mature or profession stage.

•Cooperative Learning: Web-based entertainment and cooperative stages urge distributed picking up, encouraging networks of students who share assets, thoughts, and backing.

•Information Driven Experiences: Learning investigation give bits of knowledge into students' advancement and commitment, empowering more successful mediations and backing.

Challenges in the Computerized Age

•Data Over-burden: The tremendous measure of data accessible online can be overpowering, making it hard to perceive dependable sources from falsehood.

•Advanced Interruption: The consistent presence of computerized gadgets can prompt interruptions, decreasing the viability of learning and debilitating fixation.

•Computerized Separation: In spite of advances in innovation, variations in admittance to advanced apparatuses and the web persevere, worsening instructive imbalances.

Systems for Powerful Computerized Learning

•Creating Computerized Proficiency: Basic abilities incorporate assessing the validity of online sources, grasping advanced freedoms as well as expectations, and exploring computerized apparatuses really.

•Overseeing Computerized Interruptions: Methods, for example, laying out unambiguous objectives, utilizing time usage instruments, and establishing a favorable learning climate can assist with limiting interruptions.

•Encouraging Computerized Wellbeing: Adjusting screen time with disconnected exercises and rehearsing advanced care can uphold mental and actual wellbeing in the computerized age.

Utilizing Innovation for Improved Learning

•Mixed Getting the hang of: Consolidating on the web computerized media with conventional homeroom strategies offers a decent methodology that use the qualities of the two conditions.

•MOOCs and Online Courses: Gigantic Open Web-based Courses (MOOCs) and other internet learning stages give potential chances to getting to excellent schooling from establishments all over the planet.

•Instructive Applications and Devices: An assortment of applications and computerized instruments support advancing across disciplines, offering assets for training, investigation, and content creation.

Learning in the computerized age brings both exceptional open doors and difficulties. By getting it and exploring these intricacies, students can bridle advanced apparatuses to improve their instructive encounters and accomplish their learning objectives. This part stresses the significance of computerized education, careful commitment with innovation, and key utilization of advanced assets to help powerful and significant learning in the present interconnected world.

Chapter 9: Lifelong Learning and Brain Aging

As we explore through various phases of life, the idea of deep rooted learning turns out to be progressively huge, for individual and expert improvement as well as a system to balance the impacts of maturing on the cerebrum. This section investigates the effect of constant learning on keeping up with mental capability and moderating the regular downfall that accompanies maturing.

The Significance of Deep rooted Learning

Deep rooted learning alludes to the continuous, willful, and self-roused quest for information for one or the other individual or expert reasons. Past gaining explicit abilities or information, long lasting learning encourages flexibility, versatility, and an inquisitive and dynamic brain. Participating in deep rooted learning exercises has been displayed to have various advantages for more seasoned grown-ups, including further developed memory, better profound guideline, and expanded sensations of joy and satisfaction.

The Maturing Cerebrum

Maturing is related with different changes in cerebrum design and capability, remembering decreases for mind volume, changes in synapse frameworks, and the reduced capacity of neurons to successfully impart. While these progressions can influence mental capabilities, like memory, consideration, and critical thinking, research in brain adaptability and mental hold hypothesis proposes that participating in intellectually animating exercises can help keep up with and even work on mental capability in more established grown-ups.

Mental Save

Mental save alludes to the cerebrum's capacity to make do and find elective approaches to finishing jobs when confronted with difficulties. A higher mental hold is related with a lower hazard of mental deterioration and can be developed through schooling, participating in mentally animating exercises, and keeping a socially dynamic way of life.

Systems for Advancing Deep rooted Learning

•Different Learning Exercises: Participating in various mentally invigorating exercises, like learning another dialect, playing instruments, or taking up new leisure activities, can improve mental adaptability and imagination.

•Social Commitment: Taking part in bunch classes, clubs, or online networks can give social communication and daily reassurance, which are advantageous for psychological well-being and mental capability.

•Actual Activity: Ordinary active work, particularly vigorous activities, has been displayed to further develop mind wellbeing, increment cerebrum volume in basic regions, and advance neurogenesis.

•Solid Way of life Decisions: A reasonable eating regimen wealthy in cell reinforcements and omega-3 unsaturated fats, satisfactory rest, and stress the board rehearses support mind wellbeing and mental capability.

Innovation and Deep rooted Learning

Innovation assumes an essential part in working with long lasting learning. Online courses, augmented reality encounters, and computerized stages offer available and adaptable learning potential open doors for people, everything being equal. These advances can give customized growth opportunities, permitting students to investigate subjects of revenue at their own speed and level of skill.

Deep rooted learning is an integral asset for upgrading mental capability and enhancing one's life at whatever stage in life. By embracing the standards of deep rooted learning, people can advance cerebrum wellbeing, keep up with mental capacities, and partake in a satisfying and drew in life well into more established age. This section highlights the significance of ceaseless learning and gives useful techniques to people to remain mentally dynamic, socially associated, and truly solid, consequently supporting mind wellbeing and mental imperativeness all through the maturing system.

Chapter 10: Practical Applications and Case Studies

In the last meaningful part of our investigation into mental ability, learning, and memory, we dive into certifiable applications and contextual analyses. These accounts and models enlighten how the standards and systems examined all through the book can be really applied to upgrade learning, further develop memory, and keep up with mental wellbeing across different settings and phases of life.

Contextual analysis 1: Long lasting Learning in Retirement

Foundation: Maria, a 68-year-old resigned teacher, chose to devote her retirement years to long lasting learning. She left on an excursion to learn new dialects and investigate various societies through movement and online courses.

Systems Applied:

•Different Learning Exercises: Maria signed up for online language courses and partook in social trade programs.

•Social Commitment: She joined a neighborhood book club and a language trade meetup to rehearse her new dialect abilities and offer her encounters.

•Actual Activity: Maria coordinated standard strolls and yoga into her daily schedule to help her mental capability.

Result: Maria announced enhancements in her memory and mental deftness. She additionally experienced expanded sensations of satisfaction and connectedness with individuals from different foundations.

Contextual analysis 2: Executing Viable Learning Strategies in Schooling

Foundation: A secondary school in a medium-sized city presented another learning system in view of the successful learning procedures illustrated in Part 5 to upgrade understudies' comprehension and maintenance of data.

Techniques Applied:

•Dispersed Redundancy and Dynamic Review: Educators carried out separated reiteration in their example designs and energized dynamic review through successive, low-stakes tests.

•Elaborative Cross examination: Understudies were urged to shape concentrate on bunches where they could ask and reply "how" and "why" questions connected with the material.

•Double Coding: Examples were upgraded to incorporate visual guides close by verbal guidance.

Result: After a semester, understudies showed huge enhancements in their grades and in general cognizance of the material. Criticism from understudies additionally demonstrated expanded commitment and satisfaction in the educational experience.

Contextual investigation 3: Combatting Age-Related Mental degradation

Foundation: John, a 75-year-old resigned engineer, started seeing gentle memory passes and chose to find proactive ways to keep up with his mental wellbeing.

Techniques Applied:

•Deep rooted Learning: John took up chess and began figuring out how to play the piano, exercises known to invigorate mental capability.

•Actual Activity: He integrated lively strolling into his day to day daily practice.

•Sound Way of life Decisions: John changed his eating routine to incorporate more mind good food varieties, like fish wealthy in omega-3 unsaturated fats, berries, and green verdant vegetables.

Result: Throughout a year, John noticed upgrades in his memory, state of mind, and in general feeling of prosperity. He likewise found himself all the more socially dynamic and drawn in with his local area.

These contextual analyses highlight the functional appropriateness of the ideas examined all through this book. Whether through upgrading schooling, advancing retirement, or fighting mental degradation, the methodologies of viable learning, way of life decisions, and a comprehension of the cerebrum's capacities can significantly affect our lives. By embracing these standards, people, everything being equal, can open their full mental potential, accomplish their learning objectives, and partake in a lively, mentally satisfying life.

As we finish up this part, obviously the excursion to improving mental ability and boosting learning and memory is both profoundly private and generally important. This present reality applications and victories shared here act as motivation and demonstration of the extraordinary force of embracing long lasting learning, vital mental practices, and solid way of life decisions.

Reflecting on the Journey

We left on this investigation fully intent on opening the privileged insights of mental ability, diving into the perplexing components of learning and memory. From the essential study of the cerebrum to the significant systems for mental upgrade, every part has contributed a part of the riddle of how we can saddle our mental potential.

The Study of the Mind

Our process started with an investigation of the mind's life systems and capabilities, laying the basis for understanding how learning and memory are worked with on a natural level. The ideas of brain adaptability and the cerebrum's dynamic limit with respect to change arose as focal subjects, offering expectation and inspiration for those trying to upgrade their mental capacities.

Techniques for Improving Learning and Memory

The core of our investigation dove into reasonable techniques for expanding learning and further developing memory maintenance. Procedures like divided redundancy, dynamic review, and elaborative cross examination were hypothetical ideas as well as instruments that, when applied, can fundamentally upgrade our learning proficiency and adequacy. In addition, the conversation reached out past individual endeavors, featuring the effect of way of life factors and the significance of close to home and persuasive aspects in the educational experience.

Application in Day to day existence and Then some

Maybe most convincing were this present reality applications and contextual investigations that rejuvenated the standards talked about. These stories showed that the methodologies for improving mental ability are not restricted to scholastic or disconnected pursuits yet are profoundly pertinent to different parts of day to day existence, from self-improvement in retirement to imaginative instructive methodologies and systems for alleviating age-related mental degradation.

Key Bits of knowledge

•The Cerebrum's Flexibility: Understanding brain adaptability enables us to embrace ways of life and take part in exercises that advance mental development and strength.

•Comprehensive Way to deal with Learning: Compelling learning isn't exclusively about scholarly commitment yet additionally includes overseeing way of life factors, profound states, and inspirational drives.

•Long lasting Learning: The quest for information and new encounters shouldn't lessen with age but instead go on as a deep rooted try to keep up with mental imperativeness and improve life's excursion.

Future Bearings

As we stand on the cliff of arising exploration and advances, the field of mental upgrade is ready with potential. Headways in neuroscience, computerized learning stages, and customized schooling vow to additionally change our comprehension and abilities. The investigation of cerebrum PC interfaces, expanded reality for instructive purposes, and man-made intelligence driven customized opportunities for growth are only the skyline of what's conceivable.

Last Considerations

The excursion through "Intellectual prowess: Opening the Privileged insights of Learning and Memory" has been one of revelation, not simply of the capacities of the human mind yet of the potential inside every one of us to upgrade our mental capacities and personal satisfaction. It is a source of inspiration, an update that we are not detached beneficiaries of our mental limits but rather dynamic members in forming them.

As you close this book, may you convey forward the interest, methodologies, and experiences acquired into your day to day routine. Whether through taking on new learning procedures, embracing a better way of life, or participating in long lasting learning, the way to opening your mind's maximum capacity is both an individual and aggregate excursion. Allow us to keep on investigating, learn, and develop, for chasing after information lies the ability to change ourselves and our general surroundings.

Much thanks to you for setting out on this excursion through the pages of this book. May it be a venturing stone to a future where the privileged insights of learning and memory keep on unfurling, enlightening ways to more prominent figuring out, development, and satisfaction.

Appendix A: Glossary of Terms

This part characterizes key terms utilized all through the book, giving perusers a fast reference to comprehend the logical and instructive ideas connected with intellectual prowess, learning, and memory.

- Cognitive Neuroscience: The study of how brain function is related to thinking, learning, and memory processes.
- Neuroplasticity: The ability of the brain to change and adapt in response to new experiences, learning, or injury.
- Cognitive Reserve: The mind's resistance to damage of the brain. It explains why some individuals with brain pathology maintain cognitive function, while others with similar pathology exhibit memory and thinking deficits.
- Spaced Repetition: A learning technique that involves increasing intervals of time between subsequent review of previously learned material to exploit the psychological spacing effect.
- Active Recall: A practice where learners actively stimulate their memory during the learning process by testing themselves on the material they are trying to learn.
- Elaborative Interrogation: A method that enhances learning by asking "how" and "why" questions to deepen understanding of the subject matter.
- Interleaved Practice: A practice strategy that involves mixing different topics or forms of material within a single study session.

Appendix B: Recommended Reading and Resources

To further explore the topics of brain power, learning, and memory, this section lists books, articles, and online resources that offer deeper insights and additional strategies.

Books

- "Make It Stick: The Science of Successful Learning" by Peter C. Brown, Henry L. Roediger III, and Mark A. McDaniel - A comprehensive guide to effective learning strategies backed by scientific research.
- "The Brain That Changes Itself: Stories of Personal Triumph from the Frontiers of Brain Science" by Norman Doidge - An exploration of neuroplasticity and the brain's capacity for change.
- "Mindset: The New Psychology of Success" by Carol S. Dweck - Discusses the impact of fixed and growth mindsets on learning and success.

Online Resources

- Coursera and edX: Platforms offering courses on a wide range of topics, including cognitive science and psychology, from leading universities.
- Anki and Quizlet: Tools for implementing spaced repetition and active recall through flashcards.
- TED Talks: Inspirational talks on education, cognitive science, and personal development.

Appendix C: Useful Apps and Technologies for Learning

This section highlights several apps and technologies designed to support various learning strategies, enhance memory, and promote brain health.

- Duolingo: A language learning app that uses spaced repetition and gamification to make learning new languages fun and effective.
- Lumosity: A brain training app offering games designed to improve memory, attention, flexibility, speed of processing, and problem-solving skills.
- Headspace: An app providing guided meditation and mindfulness practices, beneficial for stress management and cognitive function.

Conclusion of Appendices

The informative supplements give an establishment to additional investigation and ceaseless advancing past the center substance of this book. By using the glossary for speedy reference, drawing in with the suggested readings and assets, and consolidating valuable applications and advancements into their learning methodologies, perusers are prepared to proceed with their excursion toward opening the maximum capacity of their mental ability. This tool stash not just supplements the experiences shared all through the book yet additionally urges perusers to seek after a deep rooted obligation to learning, mental upgrade, and by and large mind wellbeing.

www.ingramcontent.com/pod-product-compliance
Lightning Source LLC
Chambersburg PA
CBHW021400160726
47994CB00007B/3030